Life is full *of* Choices – choose wisely!

———— Philip O. Akinyemi

All Scriptures are taken from the New King James Version of the Bible, Copyright © 1982 by Thomas Nelson, Inc. Used by permission. All rights reserved.

Averting the Consequences of Our Sin

Then they journeyed from Mount Hor by the Way of the Red Sea, to go around the land of Edom; and the soul of the people became very discouraged on the way. And the people spoke against God and against Moses: "Why have you brought us up out of Egypt to die in the wilderness? For there is no food and no water, and our soul loathes this worthless bread." So the LORD sent fiery serpents among the people, and they bit the people; and many of the people of Israel died. Therefore the people came to Moses, and said, "We have sinned, for we have spoken against the LORD and against you; pray to the LORD that He take away the serpents from us." So Moses prayed for the people. Then the LORD said to Moses, "Make a fiery serpent, and set it on a pole; and it shall be that everyone who is bitten, when he looks at it, shall live." So Moses made a bronze serpent, and put it on a pole; and so it was, if a serpent had bitten anyone, when he looked at the bronze serpent, he lived. (Numbers 21:4-9).

Numbers 21 marks the end of the journeys of the children of Israel to the Promised Land. They were long, tiresome, arduous wanderings that had lasted close to thirty-nine years. The first journey was from the Red Sea to Sinai (Exodus 13-19), and that was between April 14, 1445, and May 1, 1444 BC.[1] The second journey was from Sinai to Kadesh (Numbers 11-12), and the subsequent wilderness wandering due to their disobedience and rebellion against God. The third and last journey started on September 1, 1406 BC, at Mount Hor. Aaron and most of the first generation that was disobedient to God had perished in their harsh desert surroundings, and never gained entrance into the Promised Land. A new era began with a new high priest, Eleazar, the son of Aaron. This new era commenced with God giving them

---

1 Ellisen, Stanley, *Knowing God's Word: Interpretive Charts and Outlines of the Old Testament*, p. 38.

a great victory over King Arad the Canaanite (21:1-3). However, this new generation had to relearn many of the lessons of the first concerning the consequences of murmuring and unbelief. This moved God to send poisonous serpents among His people.

An important lesson from this chapter is that "the consequences of one's sin can be averted only by the means which God provides." This is a reverberating theme throughout the entire Bible. From the fall of man in Genesis 3 to the great white throne judgment in Revelation 20, the Bible shows that God has provided a means of escaping the repercussions of sin, but the choice of whether to accept God's terms has always been left to mankind.

Israel's Sin:

What led to Israel's sin? Frustration! Frustration arises when there is a delay or perceived resistance to the fulfillment of our desires or goals. Uncurbed frustration will lead to discouragement and doubt. In verse 4, we are told that the people were discouraged because of the journey. Then the people started speaking against God and against Moses: *"Why have you brought us up out of Egypt to die in the wilderness? For there is no food and no water, and our soul loathes this worthless bread."* Right here, they demeaned God's provision of heavenly manna that they didn't have to work for; they never had to grow grain (wheat), harvest it, grind it, or bake it. They called God's provision "worthless bread."

Are you appreciative of God's provisions, or you are taking them for granted? When we should be thanking and praising God, we are sometimes ungrateful and complain. The air we breathe is given to us freely, as are the rain and the sunshine that cause our crops to grow. There is no way in a million years that we could pay for them. Therefore, let us be thankful unto the Lord.

For nearly forty years, Israel had been itching to enter this land flowing with milk and honey, and they were so close. But the Edomites denied them passage through their land. This, of course, would have shortened their journey and expedited their entrance into the Promised Land; instead they had to go around the land of Edom, and the souls of the people became dejected. They reverted to their familiar way of venting their frustration by murmuring and complaining. *"Why have you brought us up out of Egypt to die in the wilderness?"* (Exodus 14:11, 17:3; Numbers 11:20, 14:2, 20:4, 21:5).

Since none of us is immune to frustration, what should we do when it comes?

1. Calm down. The Bible says, *"Be still, and know that I am God"* (Psalm 46:10). Sometimes frustration comes when we focus on ourselves. Remember, joy comes when you put Jesus first, others second, and yourself last.

2. Go to the throne of grace in prayer, because there you will obtain mercy and find grace (Hebrews 4:16). Grace gives you empowerment to deal with every situation.

3. Submit to the Holy Spirit as He guides you: do not lean on your own understanding (Proverbs 3:5-6).

4. Give thanks to God. Believe that all things work together for good to them that love Him, to them who are called according to his purpose (Romans 8:28). *"In everything give thanks"* (1 Thessalonians 5:18).

Doubt:

If you do not get rid of frustration, it will lead to doubt. Israel doubted God's protection and provision. Had they forgotten so quickly who parted the Red Sea before them? While they walked safely through the sea, their enemies perished! Or who rained down manna freely for them to feed? How about the water that came out of the rock at Meribah? How about the victories over their enemies, who outnumbered them and probably had better weapons? How about the ten plagues of Egypt, and how they were set free from Egyptian slavery? Who did all these things for them? Didn't they remember that it was the God of their fathers, Abraham, Isaac, and Jacob, the true and living God? And if they were to perish in the wilderness, would He have asked them to leave Egypt?

However, before we point accusing fingers, we must look into our own lives and see where we sometimes doubt because of delays. How about when you are embarking on a journey and doubts fill your mind about whether you will be safe? Have you forgotten that the God who keeps you does not sleep nor slumber? Or have you feared that your business was going under, forgetting that God who gave you success in the past years doesn't change? Has doubt come into your heart when you see the ministry you labored over not growing according to your expectations? Is God not the One who gives the increase? The apostle Paul said, *"I planted, Apollos watered, but God gave the increase"* (1 Corinthians 3:6). Has doubt set in that your children will not turn out the way you have trained them? How about Isaiah 54:13, where God promised, *"All your children shall be taught by the LORD, And great shall be the peace of your children"*? Or regarding your health, how about God's word to you that says, *"I am the*

LORD *who heals you"* (Exodus 15:26); and also His promise, *"For I will restore health to you"* (Jeremiah 30:17)? If you are going through several afflictions, remember Psalm 34:19, *"Many are the afflictions of the righteous, But the LORD delivers him out of them all,"* and Hebrews 13:5, *"I will never leave you nor forsake you."*

Dealing with Doubt:

I believe the only One who ever walked this planet without an iota of doubt was Jesus Christ. We all have doubts at some point, but we must promptly get rid of them. Rev. Billy Graham said, "You cannot prevent a bird from flying over your head, but you can prevent it from making a nest on your head." It is our responsibility to cast out doubts from our minds.

Even John the Baptist, whom Jesus described in Matthew 11:11 as the greatest born of women, had doubts. He sent two of his disciples to Jesus to ask Him if He was the Messiah to come or if they should still be expecting someone else. Remember, John had baptized Jesus at the River Jordan; he had seen the heavens open and the Spirit of God descend like a dove to light upon Jesus, and heard a voice from heaven saying, *"This is My beloved Son, in whom I am well pleased"* (Matthew 3:17). And in John 1:29, it was the same John the Baptist who said, *"Behold! The Lamb of God who takes away the sin of the world!"* So what happened? At this time, John was imprisoned by Herod because he criticized him for marrying his brother's wife. John had been chosen by God for the ministry of preparing the way before the Lord Jesus, but had barely started when he was thrown into prison.

This, of course, had to be frustrating to John and make him wonder if Jesus was really the One to deliver Israel. What was Jesus' response? *"Go and tell John the things you have seen and heard: that the blind see, the lame walk, the lepers are cleansed, the deaf hear, the dead are raised, the poor have the gospel preached to them"* (Luke 7:22). Why did Jesus not respond directly by saying, "Yes, I am the One," but instead refer him to Scriptures about what the prophets said concerning Him (Isaiah 35:5-6)? I believe Jesus is teaching us here that when we are in doubt, we should turn to the Word of God.

What can we learn from John's approach to doubts?

1. Talk to Jesus through your prayers, and the Holy Spirit who lives in you will guide you.
2. Go back to His Word, the Bible, and if you are still not clear, talk to a minister or an elder in Christ.

Unbelief:

Unbelief manifests itself in the form of doubts. Charles Spurgeon referred to unbelief as "Satan's first-born child." It is the instrument of Satan that works well for him on people. It was what he used on Eve in the Garden: *"Has God indeed said, 'You shall not eat of every tree of the garden'?"* As their conversation continued, the devil said unto her, *"You will not surely die,"* contrary to the command of God.

Unbelief is sin, and it will rob you of God's blessing. Imagine you are a father, and you told your ten-year-old child that you would buy him a bicycle. He looked you in the eye and said, "I don't believe you," or "I doubt you." How would you feel? Would you be excited to go to the store and purchase a bicycle immediately for him? When God says He will provide and protect us and we doubt Him, we are doing exactly what the ten-year-old boy did.

Unbelief can also destroy a man. In 2 Kings 7, we read the account of the lord on whom the king leaned who expressed his disbelief in God's promise, which led to his death. He was trodden down in the streets of Samaria and died as a result of unbelief. There was great famine in Samaria because the Syrian army besieged the city, to the extent that two women had to boil a child for a meal. When the king heard from the woman whose child was eaten, he became enraged and vowed to kill Elisha, because he felt Elisha could do something about the situation in the city.

Elisha sent a message from the Lord that by the next day, flour and barley, which were scarce and expensive would be in abundance and sold at a cheap price at the gates of Samaria. But the officer doubted the word of God from Elisha and said, *"If the LORD would make windows in heaven, could this thing be?"* (v. 2). The prophet Elisha replied, *"You shall see it with your eyes, but you shall not eat of it."* The words of Elisha came to pass just as he had pronounced. The officer saw the abundant food, but he was trodden down and perished at the gate because of unbelief. This man must have seen and heard some of the great things God had done through Elisha: how the Shunamite woman's son was raised from the dead; how Elisha revealed the secrets of the king of Syria, Benhadad, and struck his army with blindness, and led them to Samaria before the king of Israel; and the cure of Naaman's leprosy. Despite all these miracles, he disbelieved the word of God from Elisha. Unbelief can surely destroy a man.

The Bible records two things that Jesus marveled at. These two things are diametrically opposite to each other. The first is faith and the second unbelief. When Jesus entered into Capernaum, a centurion (Gentile) whose servant was sick with palsy came beseeching Him to heal his servant. Jesus told him, I will come and heal him, but the centurion said to Jesus, You do not need to come to my house, just speak the word only. Jesus was astonished at his faith-filled words and said, *"Assuredly, I say to you, I have not found such great faith, not even in Israel!"* (Matthew 8:10). On the other hand, when Jesus got to His own hometown, we are told He could not do mighty works there and only a few sick folk were healed, and Jesus marveled because of their unbelief (Mark 6:6). For us to receive blessings from God, we have an important part to play: we must believe His Word.

Repercussions:

Our actions always have repercussions. If you steal and you are caught, you will pay a penalty for it. The punishment is meant to deter you from continuing in such disgraceful behavior and teach others not to do the same. If sin is not punished, others will feel justified in carrying out the same behavior. That is why the apostle Paul so rightly declared, *"Now all these things happened to them as examples, and they were written for our admonition, upon whom the ends of the ages have come"* (1 Corinthians 10:11). God had to discipline Israel for their sin. However, when they realized their sin, they repented and asked Moses to intercede for them. *"Therefore the people came to Moses, and said, 'We have sinned, for we have spoken against the LORD and against you; pray to the LORD that He take away the serpents from us.' So Moses prayed for the people"* (21:7).

No matter how many times we miss the mark, God is always willing to forgive us and wash us clean. In 1 John 1:9, we read, *"If we confess our sins, He is faithful and just to forgive us our sins and to cleanse us from all unrighteousness."* The Psalmist says, *"As far as the east is from the west, So far has He removed our transgressions from us"* (Psalm 103:12). God devised a means to heal the Israelites by asking Moses to make a brazen serpent and lift it up, saying that anyone bitten by the fiery serpent when he or she looked up to it would live and not die.

The repercussions of sin can be avoided if we believe God's Word and His means of salvation. *"How shall we escape if we neglect so great a salvation?"* (Hebrews 2:3). Healing depends on individual choice and faith in the Word of God!

Redemption:

After Israel repented, God provided a means to redeem them from death by snakebite. The brazen serpent foreshadowed the redemption of the human race that was to come. Jesus would later draw an analogy between His cross and the brazen serpent Moses raised on a pole in John 3:14-15: *"And as Moses lifted up the serpent in the wilderness, even so must the Son of Man be lifted up;*

that whoever believes in Him should not perish but have eternal life."

There are many similarities that can be drawn between the two. Just as the serpent was God's means of bringing physical healing to the Israelites (Numbers 21:8), so Jesus is God's means of physical and spiritual healing for the human race (Isaiah 53:5; John 3:16; 1 Peter 2:24). Just as the serpent represented a cursed creature (Genesis 3:14) that later came to symbolize life, likewise Christ became a curse for us that we may live eternally (Galatians 3:13). Just as the serpent had to be lifted up in the wilderness to enable the believing Israelites to look and be healed (Numbers 21:9), the Son of Man had to be crucified on the cross so that those who believed in Him could receive eternal life (John 12:32). The healing power of the brazen snake lay not in magic, but in faith. Similarly, the healing power of Jesus lies in believing God's Word about the meaning of His death.

Choice:

A common saying in our home, especially by my wife when our children were younger, was "Life is full of choices," and she would add, "Choose wisely!" This is a true statement. Where you are today hinges principally on the choices you made yesterday. Our world today is full of choices: what clothes to wear, what food to eat, and even where we want to be buried. Sometimes our choices are based on our felt needs rather than our actual needs, and the greater part of our decision process is driven by desire. Our desires are influenced by several things, such as the company we keep and the daily advertisements we are bombarded with, especially on television.

The company we keep influences the choices we make. Some young people plunge themselves into sinful and destructive habits such as drugs, fornication, and alcohol because of the groups they join.

In 2 Kings 5, we read the narrative of a Syrian military commander called Naaman. He was a leper, and came to Israel because his wife's maid had mentioned the healing he could receive from the prophet of God in Israel. Elisha told him to go and wash himself in the River Jordan seven times for healing. Naaman became wroth because his perceived method of healing was not what the man of God prescribed. He said, *"I thought, He will surely come out to me, and stand, and call on the name of the LORD his God, and strike his hand over the place, and recover the leper."* He even argued that the rivers of Damascus were better than the rivers of Israel and asked why Elisha could not have sent him to the rivers in his own country. Naaman would have missed his healing if not for the people with him, who persuaded him to choose God's means and terms for restoration.

Someone once said, "Tell me who your friends are, and I will tell you who you are." The people we keep company with are very important. Choose your friends wisely!

The Israelites in our passage had a choice: to live by looking up at the lifted brazen serpent or to die by ignoring God's means for healing. They had nothing to do with the way they were healed, but due to unbelief, some wasted their time looking for alternatives. Those who doubted God's method of healing and followed their previous knowledge of treating snakebite perished. God's methods may not make sense to us, but they are the only way to be saved. Paul says, *"For the message of the cross is foolishness to those who are perishing, but to us who are being saved it is the power of God"* (1 Corinthians 1:18).

Eternal Choice:

The choices we make such as what car to drive, where to live, or which college to attend have no eternal consequences; we can change these choices as much as we like while we still have breath. However, there exists a choice that, once made, has eternal consequences and cannot be changed after death: *"In the place where the tree falls, there it shall lie"* (Ecclesiastes 11:3).

This choice is whether or not to accept God's means of averting the consequences of our sin. The path to everlasting life is only through Jesus Christ. The Bible says, *"The soul who sins shall die"* (Ezekiel 18:4). And all have sinned (Romans 3:23). Also, the wages of sin is death, but the gift of God is eternal life in Christ Jesus our Lord (Romans 6:23). Jesus also said, *"I am the way, the truth, and the life. No one comes to the Father except through Me"* (John

14:6). God's salvation for humanity comes only through His Son Jesus Christ. To avoid eternal death, the penalty for sin, you must believe in God and His means of reconciliation.

There exists within man the pride to act independently of God by devising his own way of reaching Him. There are some who do it by following other religions such as Hinduism, Islam, or Buddhism, all claiming they are ways to heaven. But there is only one way to reach the true and living God, and that is through Jesus Christ. The Bible says, *"Nor is there salvation in any other, for there is no other name under heaven given among men by which we must be saved"* (Acts 4:12). There are some people who trust in their good works or charitable donations to lead them to heaven. As noble as these acts may be, they are not God's means of salvation. God has determined that faith in Jesus is the way to enter heaven. If we choose another path or no path at all, the end result is the same: eternal death.

For the Israelites, God's means to heal them was the brazen serpent. If anyone chose a different way, they died.

Even among church people, there are some who believe God is too good to send people to the lake of fire. Remember, the choice is yours, and as long as you have breath, there is hope if you believe in Jesus. God declared in His Word, *"I have set before you life and death, blessing and cursing: therefore choose life"* (Deuteronomy 30:19). You can only make one choice; there is nothing in between. Life or death; heaven or hell. It is not what you think or how you perceive it should be done: it is what the Word of God says.

I heard Dr. David Jeremiah on television telling the story of a lady who came to him after his preaching, saying, "My God would never send someone to hell for simply not believing in Jesus." She probably thought Dr. Jeremiah would debate her statement or go through the Bible again to show her proofs. But he calmly answered her, "You're right, your God wouldn't do that, because he doesn't exist." What a wise response! There is only one God, and any other gods you create in your mind do not exist. Whatever the living God says in His Word is the truth. *"Forever, O LORD, Your word is settled in heaven"* (Psalm 119:89). Choose wisely! Choose Jesus Christ and live eternally with God.

Please Say This Prayer with Me:

Dear God, I realize I have sinned against You, for all have sinned. I repent of my sins. Please forgive me. I commit my life to You. I want to know You more and serve You with my whole heart. I ask for Your abundant grace to always trust in You no matter the situation. I thank You, Lord, for hearing my prayer, since I prayed in the name of Jesus Christ. Amen.

What can wash away my sin?
Nothing but the blood of Jesus:
What can me whole again?
Nothing but the blood of Jesus.

   Oh! Precious is the flow
   That makes me white as snow;
   No other fount I know,
   Nothing but the blood of Jesus

For my cleansing this I see—
Nothing but the blood of Jesus!
For my pardon this my plea—
Nothing but the blood of Jesus!

Nothing can my sin erase
Nothing but the blood of Jesus!
Naught of works, 'tis all of grace—
Nothing but the blood of Jesus!

This is all my hope and peace—
Nothing but the blood of Jesus!
This is all my righteousness—
Nothing but the blood of Jesus!

                By Robert Lowry

About the Author. Dr. Philip O. Akinyemi is a father and grandfather whose beloved wife Rachel now rests in the bosom of Jesus Christ. He is an ordained minister who has served as an assistant pastor and a radio Bible teacher. He holds a doctorate in mechanical engineering from the University of Detroit and a master's degree in theological studies from Michigan Theological Seminary. He has worked for Ford Motor Company as a technical expert and served as an adjunct at the University of Detroit and Lawrence Technological University, Michigan. He currently resides with his son in the Pittsburgh area of Pennsylvania.

OTHER TITLE BY PHILIP O. AKINYEMI

The Holy Spirit

Do you know the Holy Spirit is your loving and faithful Comforter in time of sorrow? He is a divine Person who is available 24/7 to help you. Jesus the Son of God depended utterly upon the Holy Spirit in His earthly ministry, and we must do likewise in order to be effective and successful in our calling in life.

ISBN: 978-1-60383-524-4
You can get your copy at www.amazon.com
eBook at: https://www.amazon.com/Holy-Spirit-Philip-Akinyemi-ebook/dp/B01IWNJUI4

www.ingramcontent.com/pod-product-compliance
Lightning Source LLC
LaVergne TN
LVHW021746060526
838200LV00052B/3493